AR 2,9 / 0,5

Contents

The world in motion

Motion is movement. Things are in motion all around us all the time. Objects need energy to move. This energy is called a **force**. Without a force, nothing would move.

A force can be a **push** or a **pull**.

A push moves an object away.

A pull brings an object closer.

What do you think?

Is this a push or a pull force?

How do you know?

5

Are all forces the same?

Every push and pull is different. Some pushes are strong. Others are weak. A strong push will make something move farther or faster. A tugboat can push a huge cruise ship.

A horse can create a strong pull. It can pull a heavy wagon.

From one place to another

Forces also have direction. Some forces move things up or down. Other forces move things to the left or right. Some forces move things on a slanted line, called a **diagonal**.

What do you think?

Will this kick change the ball's motion? How do you know?

11

Let's get going!

Nothing will move without a pushing or pulling force. A ball on the ground will not move until a force moves it. A throw is a pushing force that moves a ball forward.

Wind is a force. It can push a beach ball through the air. Your body also has force. If you lift something, you are pulling it up.

Stop!

It takes a force to stop something that is moving. You can push something to make it stop. When you catch a football, you are using a pushing force to stop the ball.

The amount of force can change the speed of a golfball. A little push will move a golfball toward the hole. A stronger push will send it flying past the hole.

When two objects touch

All things move in a straight line unless they are pushed or pulled from a different direction. A bumper car changes direction when it hits the side of another car. The bumper car might get pushed backward. It might bounce off in a new direction.

What do you think?

This baseball is moving in a straight line. How will the ball's motion change when it is hit with the bat?

Which way will it move?

The way objects **collide**, or bump into each other, decides how their direction changes. A bowling pin hit straight on by a ball is pushed backward. A pin hit on the left side will move right. A pin hit on the right side will move left.

The speed at which object collide will also decide how their motion changes. A bowling ball that is moving slowly makes the pins fall over gently. A fast-moving ball has more force. It will knock the pins out of the way.

Moving and changing

We can see force changing motion all around us. Some objects start to move faster. Some change direction. Some come to a stop.

What do you think?

How does the motion of a puck change during a hockey game?

Words to know and Index

collide 20, 21

diagonal 8

distance 16, 17

force 4, 5, 8, 9, 10, 12, 13, 14, 16, 17, 21, 22

motion 4, 10, 11, 18, 21, 22, 23

pull 5, 6, 7, 10, 12, 13, 14

push 5, 6, 9, 10, 12, 13, 14, 16, 17, 18

speed 16, 21

Notes for adults and an activity
Activity:
Materials: Ten pennies, a smooth surface
1. Place nine pennies in a straight row on top of a smooth surface, such as a tabletop. Each penny must touch the one in front of it.
2. Place another penny about five inches (12 cm) behind the row of pennies. Invite the child to push this lead penny so that it slides into the back end of the row. What happens to the row of pennies?
3. Experiment using different amounts of force to push the lead penny into the row. Invite the child to make a curved row of pennies and repeat the experiment. Encourage the child to share their observations and ask questions about the relationship between forces, motion, and direction.
Alternative Ideas:
-Make a bowling set using recycled plastic bottles and cans.
-Use recycled paper tubes and tape to create a marble run that makes the marble move in different directions.

Learning more
Books
Amazing Forces and Movement by Sally Hewitt, Crabtree Publishing Company, 2007.
How Does it Move? by Bobbie Kalman, Crabtree Publishing, 2009.
Move It!: Motion, Forces and You by Adrienne Mason, Kids Can Press, 2005.

Websites
This PBS Kids site has video footage of motion-related experiments as well as experiments kids can try.
http://pbskids.org/dragonflytv/show/mattermotion.html
This website provides interactive learning opportunities for children to learn more about forces and movement.
http://www.bbc.co.uk/schools/scienceclips/ages/6–7/forces–movement.shtml